# THE EVEREST STORY

What is the most exciting and difficult thing in the world to do? You can run a marathon in the desert, travel around the world by bicycle, cross Antarctica on foot – the list goes on and on. But for one group of people the dream is to climb to the summit of Everest – a place where perhaps one day they can stand for a few minutes, and know that they are higher than anybody else in the world.

When the British climber George Mallory was asked why he wanted to climb Mount Everest, he said, 'Because it's there.' Many of those who come to the mountain are strong and brave, and some are lucky. But all are part of a story that has danger, success, death, and mystery at its centre. This is the story of Everest.

OXFORD BOOKWORMS LIBRARY
*Factfiles*

# The Everest Story

Stage 3 (1000 headwords)

Factfiles Series Editor: Christine Lindop

Distributed By:
Grass Roots Press
Toll Free: 1-888-303-3213
Fax: (780) 413-6582
Web Site: www.grassrootsbooks.net

TIM VICARY

# The Everest Story

OXFORD UNIVERSITY PRESS

# OXFORD
## UNIVERSITY PRESS

Great Clarendon Street, Oxford OX2 6DP

Oxford University Press is a department of the University of Oxford.
It furthers the University's objective of excellence in research, scholarship,
and education by publishing worldwide in

Oxford New York

Auckland Cape Town Dar es Salaam Hong Kong Karachi
Kuala Lumpur Madrid Melbourne Mexico City Nairobi
New Delhi Shanghai Taipei Toronto

With offices in

Argentina Austria Brazil Chile Czech Republic France Greece
Guatemala Hungary Italy Japan Poland Portugal Singapore
South Korea Switzerland Thailand Turkey Ukraine Vietnam

OXFORD and OXFORD ENGLISH are registered trade marks of
Oxford University Press in the UK and in certain other countries

ISBN: 978 0 19 4236 43 0

A complete recording of this Bookworms edition of *The Everest Story*
is available in a CD pack ISBN 978 0 19 423646 1

Printed in China

This book is printed on paper from certified and well-managed sources.

Word count (main text): 10,150

For more information on the Oxford Bookworms Library,
visit www.oup.com/bookworms

ACKNOWLEDGEMENTS
*Illustration page 4 by Peter Bull*

*The publishers would like to thank the following for permission to reproduce images*:
Mary Evans Picture Library p18 (Colonel Norton, Everest 1924/Illustrated London News Ltd);
Getty Images p49 (Himalayas Mallory Expedition 1999/Jake Norton/Mallory & Irvine); iStockphoto
pp57 (torch/Yuriy Tuchkov), 57 (climbing rope/David Morgan), 57 (rucksack/Jon Helgason), 57 (ski
poles/David Morgan), 57 (sleeping bag/Mark Herreid), 57 (climbing boots/Marek Cech), 57 (ice axe/
Jon Rasmussen); Mountain Camera Picture Library pp57 (snow goggles/John Cleare), 57 (using
oxygen/John Cleare); Reinhold Messner, pp40,42,44,45 (Everest Solo, copyright S Fisher Verlag
GmbH, Frankfurt am Main, 2000); Royal Geographical Society Picture Library pp viii(Mount
Everest 1921/A.F.R. Wollaston), 2 (George Leigh Mallory), 6 (Sir George Everest/Maull & Polyblank),
7 (Rongbuk Monastery), 9 (George Mallory and E.F. Norton/T.H. Somervell), 10 (Camp at 20,000
feet/A.F.R. Wollaston), 12 (North Col/Bentley Beetham), 14 (porters/Frank S. Smythe), 16 (Namgya
drinking tea with frost bitten hands/Bentley Beetham), 17 (Climbing the North Col/T.H. Somervell),
20 (Irvine with oxygen cylinders/Bentley Beetham), 21 (Mallory and Irvine leaving North Col for
the last climb/Noel.E. Odell), 22 (letter from Mallory/John Noel), 24 (Sherpa's/George Lowe), 26
(Khumbu Icefall/Sir Edmund Hillary), 27 (crossing crevasse/Alfred Gregory), 28 (Charles Evans &
Tom Bourdillon 1953/George Lowe), 29 (Tom Bourdillon/Charles Evans), 31 (Evans & Bourdillon/
Alfred Gregory), 33 (Edmund Hillary and Tenzing Norgay/Alfred George), 34 (The Summit ridge
of Everest untouched/Edmund Hillary), 34 (The Summit ridge of Everest with descent footprints/
Edmund Hillary), 36 (Tenzing Norgay on the Summit of Mount Everest, 1953/Edmund Hillary), 37
(Hillary and Tenzing Norgay after their ascent of Everest 1953/Alfred Gregory), 48 (Mount Everest
at sunset/Stephen Venables), 51 (1924 equipment discovered on 1999 expedition), 53 (Mount
Everest panorama/Michael Hughes); TopFoto p38 (Reinhold Messner/ullsteinbild).

# CONTENTS

# 1  The body – 1999

A group of five climbers move slowly across the north face of Everest. Suddenly, one of them sees something strange on the rocks below him. Something whiter than the snow. Carefully, he climbs down towards it. Then he calls his friends on his radio.

'Come down here,' he says. 'Look at this.'

Coming closer, they see it is the dead body of a climber. The wind has blown some of the clothes from the body, and the skin is clean and white, like new stone. In the icy cold, it looks like the body of a man who died a few days ago. But the bits of clothes that are still on the body are old, brown and grey – nothing like the brightly coloured clothes that modern climbers wear. The body is lying face down. Above the head, the fingers of one hand are dug into the icy ground. One leg is broken in two places below the knee, and the other leg is lying over it. The body looks strong and healthy, they think, like the body of a runner or dancer.

The climbers photograph the body carefully. Then, very gently, they touch the dead man's clothes – the hobnail boots, the trousers and shirt made of wool. How little he was wearing, they think, on this icy cold mountain. 'I walk out on the street in Seattle with more clothing than he had on,' one of them says. Yet here they are at 8,155 metres on Mount Everest, the highest mountain in the world.

Who is this man? He can only be one of two people, they think. But which one? Then they find a name inside his shirt. 'George Leigh Mallory', it says.

But who is George Leigh Mallory? Why are these climbers so interested in him? How did he die, and what happened to him before he died? Where is his friend, Andrew Irvine?

And the most important question of all – was this man, George Mallory, the first man to reach the summit of Everest?

George Mallory

# 2 Dangers

The climbers do not stay long with the body, because Mount Everest is one of the most dangerous places in the world. There are many things that make it difficult to stay alive here. The most important of these is the height.

The top of Everest is 8,850 metres above sea level. As you climb up the mountain, the air becomes thinner – it has less and less oxygen. Most people live less than 900 metres above sea level, where the air is full of oxygen. Above 2,000 metres the air is thinner, and people find it harder to breathe. At 4,000 metres it is harder still, and at 5,000 metres most people begin to feel ill. They get headaches, feel tired, and breathe quickly all the time, like someone who has run a long way.

In 1921, when Mallory first went to Everest, no one had climbed a mountain higher than 7,500 metres, and many people did not think it was possible. 'If climbers don't have enough oxygen, they'll be too tired to climb,' they said. 'And they won't be able to think clearly, either. So they will make stupid mistakes – forget to eat and drink, or talk to people who are not there. Perhaps they'll die.'

But the need for oxygen is not the only problem on Everest. There is also the weather. Almost every week there are winds of 100 or even 200 kph (kilometres per hour). It is difficult to walk or even stand up in these winds. The wind can blow climbers off the edge of the mountain, thousands of metres to the valley below. Climbers sometimes sit in their tents for

days, unable to sleep because of the noise, and afraid that the wind will blow their tents away.

And then there is the cold. Temperatures on Everest often fall below −20 °C, but the wind makes that feel much colder.

But before anyone can climb Everest they have to get there. Tibet in China is to the north of Everest, and Nepal is to the south, and until 1950, Nepal refused to let any foreign climbers enter their country. So the earliest climbers, like Mallory and Irvine, had to get to Everest from the north, through Tibet. And that was not easy at all.

# 3 Through Tibet to Everest – 1921

Until the early nineteenth century, nobody in the west knew about Mount Everest. People in Tibet knew, of course – they called it Chomolungma: 'Goddess Mother of the World', and to people in Nepal it was Sagarmatha: 'Goddess of the Sky'. But no one in Tibet or Nepal had ever climbed the mountain – they thought that was a very strange idea. And no foreign person had ever been so far into the Himalayas.

But in the 1830s a British soldier called George Everest was making maps in north India. He made the first maps of the Himalayas, and measured the height of some of the mountains. But Everest finished his work in 1843, and he never saw Chomolungma. The first British man to see the mountain was Everest's friend, Andrew Waugh. In 1852 Radhanath Sikdhar, who worked for Waugh, said he had discovered the highest mountain in the world. It was measured carefully many times. Then in 1856 Waugh said that this was the highest mountain in the world. He gave it the name of his old friend, George Everest, in 1865.

But very few British people were able to enter Tibet or Nepal at that time. So it was not until 1921 that the first British expedition went to see if it was possible to climb the mountain. There were nine British climbers on this expedition, and one of them was George Mallory.

To get to Everest, the climbers had to walk 500 kilometres through Tibet. Their Tibetan porters carried everything

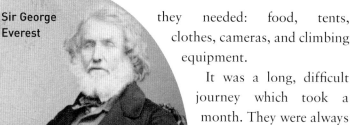

Sir George Everest

they needed: food, tents, clothes, cameras, and climbing equipment.

It was a long, difficult journey which took a month. They were always climbing – at first through river valleys with tall trees, colourful flowers and birds – then onto a wide stony place where nothing grew. There was no sound except the wind, and all the time the air was becoming thinner.

The climbers walked past Tibetan villages high up on the sides of mountains, and came to Rongbuk, the highest monastery in the world, 4,800 metres above sea level. The monks in the monastery looked at the visitors in surprise, wondering why they wanted to climb the dangerous mountain.

The climbers decided that the best way to get onto the mountain was to go up the East Rongbuk Glacier. From there they planned to climb to the North Col, a small flat place on the north ridge of Everest.

By this time it was late in the year, and the winds were getting stronger. They had not planned to get to the summit this year, but only to look for a way up. But on 23 September 1921, Mallory, with two other climbers and three porters, climbed up the steep ice wall of the East Rongbuk Glacier. When they reached the snow ridge of the North Col the next day, they could see the summit, 1,800 metres above them. But at 7,000 metres it was difficult to breathe, and they moved slowly. And they could hardly stand up in the strong icy winds.

They would have to go down, and come back next year.

**The Rongbuk Monastery and Mount Everest**

# 4 The first attempt – 1922

In 1922 a larger expedition returned. They brought oxygen with them this time, but the equipment was very heavy, and it did not always work. Many of the climbers wanted to climb the mountain on their own, if possible, without help. So climbing with oxygen was not popular with most of the climbers.

Four climbers set out on the first summit attempt – Mallory, Morshead, Norton, and Somervell. With five porters, they left Camp 4 on the North Col at 7.00 a.m. There was a terrible cold wind, and the climbers moved slowly, cutting steps in the snow for the porters behind them. They hoped to reach 8,230 metres that day, but at 7,620 metres they were too cold and tired to go on. They found a place for Camp 5 and the porters left their loads here and went back down.

The four men crawled into their two small tents to rest. But all night there was a high wind, and it was difficult to breathe or sleep. To get water to drink, they had to melt snow over a small cooker, which took a long time.

Next morning, Morshead was ill. So Mallory, Norton, and Somervell set out at 8.00 a.m., leaving Morshead alone in the tent. They moved slowly, stopping after every few steps to rest and breathe. As they climbed, their hobnail boots slipped dangerously on the stones and rocks. In the thin air they felt tired, more tired than any of them had ever felt before. At 2.00 p.m. they reached 8,227 metres,

Mallory and Norton
at 8,227 meters

but they were still about 600 metres below the summit. So they turned back, and helped Morshead down to Camp 3.

On the way down, they met three more of their climbers coming up. They were the Australian George Finch, a Gurkha called Tejbir Bura, and Geoffrey Bruce – a young man who had never climbed before. Unlike the first group, Finch and Bruce liked using oxygen. They made a new Camp 5 – 150 metres higher than Mallory's – but then they were caught in a storm and had to stay in their tent for two nights. On the third day Finch and Bruce went on, using their oxygen, to 8,323 metres. But here Bruce became exhausted and had to be helped down.

Because the oxygen had been so successful, Mallory, Somervell, and a third climber called Colin Crawford decided to make another attempt, this time with oxygen. But while they were climbing across a snow slope, there was a sudden avalanche. Everyone was buried under the snow. All the climbers and seven porters managed to climb out, but seven porters were killed.

It was clear that Everest had won – this time.

# 5     Saving the porters
# – 1924

The British climbers returned in April 1924. This time they planned to succeed. Edward Norton was the chief climber in the group of twelve men, and they had 150 Tibetan porters, both men and women, to help them. From Base Camp the porters carried equipment up to Camps 1 and 2 on the Rongbuk and East Rongbuk Glaciers. One woman carried her two-year-old child on top of an 18 kilogram load from 5,300 metres to 6,000 metres. Then she carried her child back down, and offered to go up again!

The next part was harder. On a cold, stormy day, Mallory, Irvine and two other climbers set out with twenty porters to carry equipment from Base Camp to Camp 3, but the weather was terrible. A strong wind blew down off the mountain, straight into their faces. The ice on the glacier was as clear and hard as glass. There were not enough tents at Camp 2, so some of the porters slept outside. Next morning they went on to Camp 3, but here it was even colder than before. That night the temperature fell to −29 °C. The strong icy wind blew into the tents all night, so everyone – *inside* the tents – was covered with snow.

The storm blew for two more days. Many of the porters lay in their tents, not caring about life or death. At last the storm ended and they all went down to Base Camp to rest. Three men were seriously ill; another had bad frostbite on both feet.

The porters were unhappy and afraid. 'The mountain is angry,' they said. 'It will kill us.' So on 15 May all the climbers and porters went down the valley to the Rongbuk Monastery, where the chief monk said prayers for them. Next day the wind had gone, and the sky was clear and blue.

The climbers returned to Camp 3. Then they started to climb up the steep ice wall to the North Col, to make Camp 4. And once again, things went wrong.

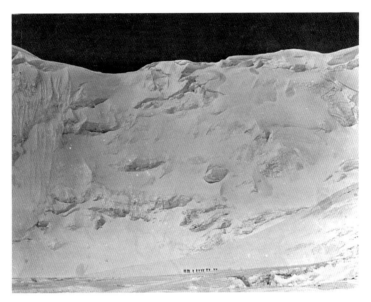

Heading for Camp 4

The ice was covered with new snow after the storm. There were many crevasses – deep holes in the ice – which were difficult to see under the snow. This was the place where seven porters had died in 1922. This time four people set out – Mallory, Norton, Odell, and Lakpa Tsering. They climbed carefully, cutting steps in the snow. They crossed several deep crevasses. Then, just below the North Col, they came to a steep slope about 100 metres high. It was a dangerous place. The slope was covered with new soft snow. At the foot of the slope was a wall of ice, falling hundreds of metres to the valley below.

Mallory climbed slowly up the slope, while Norton and Odell held him from below on a rope. After half an hour they reached the top, and found a place for Camp 4.

But all the climbers were tired. On the way down the snow suddenly collapsed under Mallory's feet and he fell into a crevasse. Only his ice axe, across the top of the crevasse, saved him. No one had seen him fall. He looked up, at the sky, then down, into the deep blue hole below him. One mistake here could mean death. Very slowly and carefully, he pulled his tired body up the ice wall and out onto the snow.

When the climbers got back to Camp 3 they were all exhausted. Their heads ached, and they coughed all night in the thin, cold air.

Next day, three more climbers – Somervell, Irvine, and Hazard – and twelve porters climbed the snow slope to Camp 4. Somervell and Irvine came down, leaving Hazard behind with the porters. That night it snowed heavily, and the temperature fell to −31 °C. The exhausted porters shivered in their tents. All next day Norton, in Camp 3, waited for them to come down. At last, he saw them coming – black dots on the snow. But only eight porters and Hazard arrived at Camp 3. Four porters had turned back, afraid that they would fall.

So now four porters were alone at Camp 4. And more and more snow was falling, making the steep slope more dangerous than ever. Without help from the climbers, the porters would die.

**To the North Col**

All the climbers were tired and ill. Mallory and Somervell had bad throats and were coughing badly. It snowed heavily all night. But next morning Norton, Mallory, and Somervell climbed slowly up towards Camp 4. It was difficult, dangerous work. They reached the snow slope, and called out to the porters above them in words like these.

'Are you alive?' the climbers asked. 'Can you walk?'

'Yes sir,' a porter answered. 'But we're afraid. It's too dangerous. If we slip, we'll fall, and die!'

'If you stay there, you'll die of cold,' Norton said. 'Wait there – we're coming to get you.'

Very carefully, Somervell climbed across the steep slope, towards the four porters. He had a rope round his waist. Mallory and Norton held the rope from below, to keep Somervell safe. But when he was five metres away from the porters, Somervell reached the end of the rope.

'What do I do now?' he thought. 'We have no more rope, and it will soon be dark.'

'Come across!' he called out to the porters. 'It's not far. Carefully, one at a time.'

The first two porters reached Somervell safely. Then they climbed past him, holding the rope, towards Norton and Mallory. Somervell looked at the last two porters.

'Come on,' he said. 'It's not difficult. One at a time.'

But the porters were afraid, and both started together. A second later they slipped and fell. They slid past Somervell down the slope, towards the valley thousands of metres below. But then, a few metres from the edge of the slope, they stopped.

'Don't move,' Somervell said. 'Just wait for me.'

He drove his ice axe deep into the snow. He untied the rope from his waist, and passed it round the head of the ice axe. Then, holding his end of the rope with one hand, Somervell climbed down until he could just reach the men with his other hand. He pulled up the first man, then the second. They climbed along the rope to Mallory and Norton. Somervell tied the rope round his waist again, and climbed back after them.

Even now they were not safe. It was nearly dark, and a long way above Camp 3. One of the porters, Namgya, could not use his hands, because he had bad frostbite. But at last they reached Camp 3, where two more climbers, Noel and Odell, were waiting with warm food.

All the climbers were exhausted. Mallory and Somervell could not stop coughing, and Norton's feet hurt badly. Helping the four porters had made them very, very tired. And they were nowhere near the summit of Everest.

Slowly they went down to Camp 1. They needed time to rest, and to decide what to do next.

**Sherpa Namgya
with bad frostbite**

# 6  Somervell and Norton – 1924

Norton decided that two pairs of climbers would try to reach the summit, without oxygen. Mallory and Geoffrey Bruce would go first, and Norton and Somervell would follow the next day. The climbers would find a place for Camp 5 above 7,600 metres, and for Camp 6 at 8,231 metres. Odell and Irvine would go up to Camp 4, to help the climbers when they came down.

On 1 June Mallory and Bruce climbed up to Camp 4 with nine porters. The next day was clear and sunny, but above the North Col they met a terrible icy wind. It was difficult to stand, hardly possible to walk. Only five porters continued with Mallory and Bruce. At 7,600 metres, they found a place for two small tents on a steep slope – Camp 5. All that night they shivered in their sleeping bags, while the wind

**Climbing the North Col**

tried to blow their tents into the air. Next morning they were all ill. Only one porter was able to go on. Sadly, they decided to come down.

As they went down, they passed Norton and Somervell with four more porters, coming up. These men reached Camp 5, and spent a better night there. The wind was less strong, and they managed to cook, eat and sleep. It was very, very cold, and in the thin air, with no oxygen, it was difficult to move. But next morning, three porters – Napboo Yishay, Lhakpa Chedi, and Semchumbi – were ready to go on.

They climbed on, up to 8,170 metres – higher than any man had been before. Here, at 1.30 p.m., they put up one tiny tent – Camp 6. Then the porters went down to the North Col, while Norton and Somervell got ready for the night. As it grew dark, they wondered: can a man sleep, without oxygen, at this height?

*Yes!* It was 'the best night since I left Camp 1,' Norton wrote. So at 6.45 next morning the two men set out for the summit. They

**Norton climbs on alone**

climbed slowly, taking three or four breaths for every step. They stayed a little below the ridge, to keep out of the wind. But in the shadow of the mountain, out of the sun, it was very cold. Norton shivered all the time, and he was having trouble with his eyes. Somervell coughed a lot, and his bad throat made it difficult to breathe.

By midday they were at 8,536 metres. The view was wonderful – they were above the clouds, with a sea of mountains below them.

But Somervell was exhausted. His throat was worse; he could hardly breathe. So Norton went on alone. He was moving more and more slowly, on a steep slope like the roof of a house. There were large stones and soft snow under his feet; it was easy to fall. And below him – 2,743 metres straight down, in the thin clear air – was the East Rongbuk Glacier and Camp 3.

He looked up. He was about 275 metres below the summit, but they were vertical metres – metres measured up the mountain, not along it. But he was tired, and moving very slowly. And his eyes were getting worse. Sometimes he saw two ice axes in his hand, not one. He knew that it was possible. He could get to the summit – but he could not get back.

Norton was nearer the summit than any man before him. But at 8,575 metres, he decided to turn back towards Somervell. It was the right thing to do. Halfway down to Camp 5, Somervell stopped. There was something in his throat – for nearly a minute he could not breathe at all. Then he coughed up a ball of blood, and could breathe again.

When they reached Camp 4, Norton could not see at all.

# 7 Mallory and Irvine – 1924

But to Norton's surprise, there were two more climbers at Camp 4 – Mallory and Irvine. Mallory had decided to try again – with oxygen this time. Irvine was young, and he had not climbed many mountains, but he understood the oxygen equipment better than anyone. So Mallory decided to climb with him.

Andrew Irvine

Setting out

On 6 June they set out for Camp 5. Eight porters carried food and oxygen. Next day they went on to Camp 6 with four porters. There, Mallory sent them back down with a note to Noel, who was filming the expedition:

*Dear Noel,*

*We'll probably start early tomorrow (8th) in order to have clear weather. It won't be too early to start looking out for us either crossing the rock band under the pyramid or going up skyline at 8.0 p.m.*[*]

*Yours ever, G. Mallory*

Behind them, Odell climbed up to Camp 5 with food to help them when they came down. Mallory left a note for him too, asking him to wait at Camp 4 the next evening. The weather was fine, he said, but the oxygen was very heavy to carry.

Odell was climbing alone, without oxygen. He spent the night at Camp 5 and then climbed up towards Camp 6. At 7,900 metres he found some very old rocks. Studying rocks was Odell's job, and the rocks that he found showed him that Everest had once been under the sea. At 12.50 p.m., the clouds cleared above him, and he could see the summit ridge of Everest. High on the ridge, he saw two tiny black dots moving on the snow. They climbed quickly, to the top of a

[*] Mallory wrote p.m. but meant a.m.

rock step near the summit. Then the clouds came back and they disappeared.

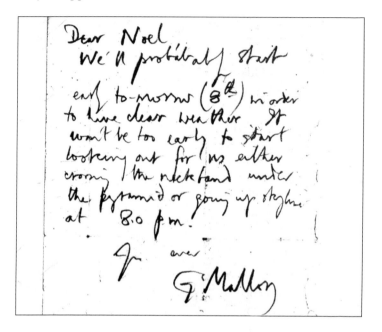

It was Mallory and Irvine, climbing strongly towards the summit. But Odell thought they were a little late. Was there enough time for them to get to the summit and then down to Camp 6 that night? He climbed up to Camp 6 and left some food for them in the tent. Then he climbed higher, towards the summit, calling out for them. But no one answered.

He wondered what to do. He wanted to stay, but the tiny tent at Camp 6 was too small for three men. So, at 4.30 p.m., he went down. By 7.00 p.m. he was in Camp 4.

The next day was 9 June. Odell was worried. When he looked up the mountain, he could see the tents of Camps 5 and 6, but nothing – and nobody – was moving. So Odell, with two porters, climbed up *again* to Camp 5.

There was a strong wind all night. The porters shivered in their tent, and next morning they refused to move. So Odell went on alone, up to Camp 6. But no one was there. The tent was closed, the food was still there. Mallory and Irvine had disappeared.

For two hours Odell climbed on, above Camp 6, towards the summit. What was he thinking? Mallory and Irvine were probably dead, but perhaps – just perhaps – one of them was still alive, badly injured up there. Perhaps he could see something, or find something, and return with some answers.

But he saw nothing, and found no bodies. Sadly, he turned back. At Camp 6, he went into the tent, and pulled out two black sleeping bags. He put them on the snow in the shape of a T. It was a message to the others, far below, that Mallory and Irvine were dead.

But what happened to them? Did they reach the summit before they died? Or did they turn back, like Norton and Somervell? No one knows.

When Odell last saw them it was already 12.50 in the afternoon. But they were moving quickly, he said. So perhaps they went on to the summit, and then were too tired to find Camp 6 before dark. Perhaps, in the darkness, one of them fell, and the other died trying to help him. Perhaps they both fell together. Or perhaps, with no more oxygen, they were just too cold and tired to move any more, and lay down in the snow to sleep.

It was seventy-five years before some of these questions were answered.

# 8  To the South Col – 1953

After 1950 Western climbers could no longer enter Tibet, but they could enter Nepal. In 1951 a British expedition went to the southern side of Everest for the first time, and in 1952 a Swiss climber called Raymond Lambert made an attempt on the summit with Tenzing Norgay. Tenzing was one of the Sherpa people of Nepal, who are excellent climbers and know the mountains well. Together Lambert and Tenzing almost reached the summit, but their oxygen equipment was not working well, and at the highest camp they had no sleeping bags. So at 8,597 metres – just a few metres higher than Norton had gone in 1924 – they turned back.

The Sherpa people of Nepal

In 1953 John Hunt came to Kathmandu, the capital of Nepal, with a large British expedition. Tenzing Norgay joined them here, and the expedition set out for Thyangboche, a monastery south of Everest. The walk took seventeen days, and 350 porters were needed to carry their equipment. In Thyangboche, they were joined by two New Zealand climbers – Edmund Hillary and George Lowe.

The climbers spent three weeks at Base Camp, getting used to the thin mountain air. They climbed smaller mountains of about 6,000 metres, learning to use the oxygen equipment. John Hunt thought that Tenzing Norgay was stronger than anyone.

Their first problem was to find a way up the Khumbu Icefall onto the Khumbu Glacier. The Khumbu Glacier is a slow-moving river of ice, and the Khumbu Icefall is a large wall of broken ice. This icefall is over 300 metres high – six times higher than Niagara Falls – and the ice in it moves, very slowly, all the time. There are pieces of ice as big as houses, which could fall on the climbers' heads at any moment. There are avalanches of ice that could kill a man in a second. Terrible crevasses go hundreds of metres down into the blue-green darkness under the climbers' feet. Sometimes the climbers heard ice moving far below them.

The climbers and Sherpas carried loads of over 18 kilograms up this difficult route. They made Camp 2 halfway up the icefall at 5,915 metres, and Camp 3 at the top of the icefall, at 6,158 metres. Then they climbed up the glacier to Camp 4 at 6,462 metres, and Camp 5 at 6,705 metres.

The next big problem was to climb the Lhotse Face to the South Col. High above Camp 5 is the mountain of Lhotse, 8,500 metres. To the left of Lhotse is the South Col of Everest. The first 600 metres of the Lhotse Face is a steep slope of

Khumbu Icefall

ice – the Lhotse Glacier. This ice is very difficult to climb, with many ice walls and deep crevasses.

For eleven long days the New Zealander George Lowe and the Sherpa Annullu fought their way up this wall of ice. All the way, they cut steps in the ice and fixed ropes for the others to follow them. They made Camp 6 at 7,010 metres, and Camp 7 at 7,315 metres. Then they began to climb to the left, across a wide snow slope, towards the South Col. But the weather was terrible, and they were very tired. High winds blew down on them from the South Col.

After twelve days of this, George Lowe was exhausted. But on 21 May, Annullu and Wilfrid Noyce finally managed to cross the difficult snow slope and reach the South Col, at 7,925 metres.

Next day, Hillary, Tenzing, and seventeen Sherpas followed them up to the South Col. The Sherpas had only a cup of tea for breakfast at Camp 7, after a long cold night.

They were carrying loads of 22 kilograms with no oxygen. At the South Col, they made Camp 8. Then, the same day, they went down again to Camp 4. They had climbed for ten hours with no food or drink all day.

But Camp 8, on the South Col, was ready at last. Now the attempt on the summit could begin.

**Crossing a crevasse**

# 9 The South Summit – 1953

On 22 May, the first two summit climbers, Tom Bourdillon and Charles Evans, set out from Camp 4 to the South Col. John Hunt and two Sherpas went with them, carrying heavy loads. Using oxygen, the three British men reached the Col first. But they were very tired, and when they took off their oxygen equipment they could not think clearly. It took them over an hour to put up a tent in the terrible wind. When the Sherpas arrived, they collapsed in the tent and could not move.

Bourdillon and Evans setting out

They rested for a day, then John Hunt and the Sherpa Da Namgyal set out to climb higher. They both had oxygen and were carrying about 20 kilograms. They moved very slowly, and Bourdillon and Evans soon came past them. Hunt and Da Namgyal both had problems with their oxygen. Sometimes ice stopped it working, and it was very difficult to breathe.

On they went, more and more slowly. At 8,338 metres Hunt and Da Namgyal could go no further. They put down their loads and turned back. When they reached the South Col, they could hardly walk.

**The final ridge**

Above them, Bourdillon and Evans went on. At 1 o'clock they reached the South Summit, 8,750 metres. In front of them they could see the final summit ridge. It was a view no man had ever seen before. To the left, a steep rocky slope fell 2,400 metres down to Camp 4 on the glacier. To the right, there was a line of white snow cornices over a drop of 2,500 metres.

Should they go on? This was their one chance to get to the top. But was it safe, or would they die, like Mallory and Irvine before them? They stood, and looked, and thought.

Evans had already had trouble with his oxygen. Bourdillon had fixed it, but they did not have a lot of oxygen left. They thought it would take three hours to reach the summit, and two hours to get back to the South Summit. By then it would be 6 o'clock, and they would have to climb down another 900 metres, without oxygen, to Camp 8. It was too far.

So, sadly, they turned back. But it was the right thing to do. The wind grew stronger, and clouds came up. It was difficult to find the way. They were very tired, and several times they slipped on the way down. At one point Evans slipped and fell. He slid past Bourdillon like a bullet, and pulled him off his feet. A moment later they were both sliding down the snow towards the glacier, thousands of feet below. Quickly, Bourdillon turned onto his face and dug his ice axe into the snow. The ice axe stopped them, but they had nearly died.

Was this what happened to Mallory and Irvine, twenty-nine years earlier? they wondered. A sudden fall, on the way down, and no one to help? It could happen so easily.

When they reached Camp 8 they were exhausted. Their faces were covered with ice, and they could hardly walk. 'They looked like strangers from another planet,' John Hunt said.

But they had climbed higher than any man before them.

Back at Camp 8

# 10 On top of the world – 1953

Hillary and Tenzing were already at Camp 8, together with John Hunt, Da Namgyal, and Ang Temba. Gregory and Lowe were there too, with three more Sherpas. But the weather was bad. A terrible wind blew straight across the South Col, and the temperature fell to −25 °C. Hillary said that it was one of the worst nights he had ever lived through.

No one could sleep. They sat shivering in their tents, hoping that the wind would not blow them away. Bourdillon and Evans were exhausted, three of the Sherpas were ill, and Hunt, like Ang Temba and Da Namgyal, had now spent three nights at 7,925 metres.

Next day, it was difficult for Bourdillon to walk, so Evans, John Hunt, and Da Namgyal helped him and Ang Temba down to Camp 7. Gregory, Lowe, and three Sherpas spent another night at Camp 8 with Hillary and Tenzing.

On the morning of 28 May the wind began to fall. Hillary and Tenzing got ready to set out. Gregory and Lowe's job was to start first and make Camp 9 somewhere below the South Summit. But two of their three Sherpas were ill, so Lowe, Gregory, and Ang Nyima carried everything between them. With their oxygen, they carried about 18 kilograms each. Hillary and Tenzing followed at 10 a.m., carrying about 22 kilograms each. Then, at 8,338 metres, they found the loads which Hunt and Da Namgyal had left, and picked them up too. Now they were carrying 27 kilograms each.

**Hillary and Tenzing**

At 2.30 p.m. they found a small place for Camp 9, at 8,506 metres. Gregory, Lowe, and Ang Nyima dropped their loads and went down. Hillary and Tenzing put up their tent, and crawled inside. The wind was very strong, and they were afraid the tent would blow away. That night, the temperature fell to −27 °C. But by 4 a.m. the wind had stopped, and the sky cleared. When they opened the tent door, in the early morning sun, they could see the monastery at Thyangboche, 4,878 metres below, where the monks were getting out of bed.

They melted snow for a warm drink, and checked the oxygen equipment carefully. Tenzing had worn his boots all night, but Hillary had taken his off, and they were as hard as ice. He had to heat them over the small cooker to make them soft.

At 6.30 a.m. they set out, and by 9 a.m. they reached the South Summit. They sat down and studied the summit ridge carefully. It looked 'frightening', Hillary thought. The snow cornices to the right were very dangerous. They were like fingers of soft snow, 2,500 metres above the valley below. And the rocks on the left looked very difficult too. But the snow just above the rocks looked better. Perhaps it was possible to climb there.

**Before the climb (left) and after (right): the first feet on the summit snow**

As soon as they stepped onto the snow, they were happy. It was good hard snow, so cutting steps in it was easy. But it was still very dangerous. One slip, and they could fall thousands of metres. Hillary went first, cutting steps in the snow. Behind him, Tenzing put the rope around his ice axe and dug it into the snow, to keep them safe. Then Hillary stopped, and Tenzing went first, cutting steps. First one man, then the other.

Several times their oxygen stopped working, and they found it hard to breathe. But each time they fixed it, and went on. As the sun rose, they felt warmer. 'To my surprise, I was enjoying the climb,' Hillary said later. The weather was still fine, and they could see the tents of Camp 4, 2,439 metres below.

But halfway up the ridge, they met a problem. They reached a rock wall, 17 metres high. It looked difficult and dangerous to climb. On the left it was clean rock; on the right, the wind had blown a cornice of hard snow against it. Hillary pushed his boot into a hole between the rock and the snow. He began to climb with his back to the rock, hoping that the snow did not move. At last he reached the top of the wall, and Tenzing followed him up.

Now, there were just 220 vertical metres to go. Slowly, cutting steps in the snow, they climbed on. Even with oxygen, they had to take two or three breaths after every step. Each time they thought they had reached the summit, they saw another one higher. They were both tired. 'The ridge seemed never-ending,' Hillary wrote later.

But then, quite suddenly, it did end. They looked around, and realised they could not go any higher. It was 11.30 a.m, and they had reached the summit of Everest.

They shook hands and threw their arms round each other.
Hillary took out a camera and took a picture – THE picture
– of Tenzing on top of Everest, the highest man in the world.
On his ice axe Tenzing had the flags of Great Britain, Nepal,
India, and the United Nations. Hillary took pictures of the
view north, south, east, and west.

Tenzing made a small hole in the snow. In it he put some
sweets, a pencil which his daughter had given him, and the
flags from the ice axe. Hillary made a hole too, and put a
small crucifix in there. They gave these things to the mountain
Chomolungma – 'Goddess Mother of the World.'

They were on top of the world – but were they really the
first men who had ever been there?

For a few minutes, Hillary and Tenzing searched, to see if Mallory and Irvine had left anything up there twenty-nine years ago. They found nothing, but that was not surprising. Every few days, there is new snow on the mountain. Every month, winds of over 150 kilometres per hour blow across the top of Everest, adding more snow, burying what was there before.

After fifteen minutes they turned back. They needed to get down before they used all the oxygen. They went carefully; it would be stupid to have an accident now. An hour later they were at the South Summit; by evening they were with George Lowe at the South Col. Next day they were down at Camp 4.

Only two men had reached the summit – one from New Zealand, one from Nepal. But everyone in the expedition was happy. They had done something no one had ever done before. But each man in the expedition had needed the help of all the others.

Down at Camp 4

# 11 One man alone – 1980

Since 1953, many hundreds of men and women have climbed Everest, most of them in large expeditions. Some groups have been very large indeed – in 1975 a Chinese expedition with 400 people managed to send nine climbers to the summit. They left a small metal tripod there, fixed to the rock. In 1985 a Norwegian expedition sent seventeen people to the top.

All these climbers, like Hillary and Tenzing, needed the help of many others. Almost all of them used oxygen, too. People have climbed Everest from the south, north, and west.

But the first climber to climb the mountain all alone, with no oxygen at all, was Reinhold Messner.

Reinhold Messner, 1995

In 1978 two climbers, Reinhold Messner and Peter
Habeler, joined a large German-Austrian expedition
climbing from Nepal. Most of the expedition were using
oxygen but Messner and Habeler decided to climb without
it. After 'the success of Hillary and Tenzing in 1953 using
oxygen,' Messner said, 'the whole world thought that this
must be the only way.'

But the early climbers did not think so. In 1924, Norton
climbed to 8,575 metres with no oxygen. So, Messner
thought, perhaps it is possible to climb 273 metres more.

He tried twice. The first time he reached the South Col
with two Sherpas, but they were caught in a terrible storm.
Their tent nearly collapsed in the wind, and they spent two
nights without eating or drinking before they came down.
But a few days later Messner tried again, with Peter Habeler,
and in ten hours they climbed from the South Col to the
summit, with no oxygen at all. But back at the South Col,
they were very ill. Habeler had a terrible headache. Messner
had taken off his goggles to make a film, and the bright snow
had hurt his eyes. Just like Norton in 1924, he lay in his tent
all night, unable to see anything. The two men needed help
to climb down from the South Col next day.

Two years later, in 1980, Messner began a new attempt.
This time he went through Tibet, like Norton and Mallory
in 1924. But Messner did not take a lot of heavy equipment
and hundreds of porters. He just went with his girlfriend,
Nena, and two Chinese people came with them to show them
the way. They started at the same place as the British Base
Camp in 1924, then, with three yaks, they climbed to Camp
3 at 6,500 metres on the East Rongbuk Glacier. Then the two
Chinese went back to Base Camp, while Nena and Messner
stayed at Camp 3 for ten days, getting used to the height.

Approaching base camp

On 24 July Messner climbed to the North Col, at 7,000 metres. But he felt very tired, and there was too much soft snow. So he and Nena returned to Base Camp and spent three weeks walking and climbing above 5,000 metres. Each day they grew stronger, and breathed more easily in the thin mountain air.

On 15 August they returned to Camp 3, and on 17 August Messner climbed up to the North Col again, much faster than before. Now he was ready, he thought. He came down to Camp 3 to sleep. That night he ate and drank, and slept for a while. Then he got up, dressed carefully, and packed his rucksack with everything he needed – food for a week, a small cooker, tent, sleeping bag, camera. He had a head torch, to see in the dark, two ski sticks, crampons, and a strong, light ice axe.

He touched Nena's face gently with his lips, and stepped out of the tent into the night.

'I shall be thinking of you,' she said sleepily. 'Bye bye.'

'Bye bye.' The words came out of the night, and then he was gone.

*\*\*\**

An hour later, he nearly died. When he was 500 metres above the camp, the snow suddenly collapsed under his feet and he fell into a crevasse. His head torch went out, and everything was dark. He had decided not to take a radio with him. Now he was frightened. He could see nothing, and it was not possible to call for help.

Then the torch came on again. He was standing on a snow bridge, about 1 metre square, above a deep black hole. He looked round. There was a small ice ridge to the left, going up. But to climb that, he needed crampons on his boots; and his crampons were in his rucksack. Very carefully, he got them out and put them on. Carefully, he reached forward across the crevasse with his arms. Then he stepped across onto the ridge – right foot first, then left. The crampons held in the ice. Slowly, he climbed up, out of the crevasse, into the night.

Far below, Nena was still sleeping in the tent.

He climbed on, up to the North Col. As the sun came out, the clouds and mountains turned from dark blue to yellow and then pink. There was good hard snow under his feet. He climbed quickly, taking fifty steps, then resting, then taking fifty more. The ski sticks made climbing easier.

As he climbed, Messner thought about Mallory and Irvine. They had come the same way up the mountain, long ago. They had oxygen, but their clothes and equipment were much heavier than Messner's. Mallory and Irvine had no light tents and sleeping bags, no crampons, no ski sticks. But when Odell last saw them, they were high up on the North Ridge. Two tiny black dots on the snow, going strongly. Did they reach the summit, he wondered. Or did they die before that?

Far below him, Nena stood outside the tent, watching Messner climb higher and higher. To her, he was now a tiny black dot on the snow. 'I would like to climb with him,' she wrote in her diary. 'One day perhaps, I tell myself . . . The further he is from me, the stronger becomes my love.'

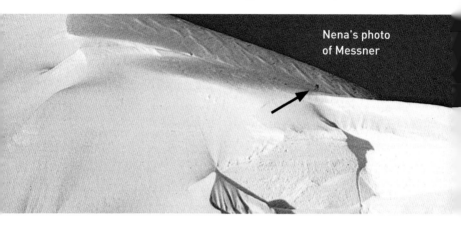

Nena's photo of Messner

By 9 a.m. Messner was at 7,360 metres. He was tired, and had to rest every thirty steps. Up here, the thin dry air had only one third as much oxygen as at sea level. His throat hurt, and for long moments he could think of nothing but breathing.

'Still a bit more, you can do it,' he told himself. 'What you climb today, you won't have to climb tomorrow.'

At last, at 7,800 metres, high up on the North Ridge, he decided to stop. The view from here was wonderful. Some of the highest mountains in the Himalayas were below him. And 1,300 metres below, he could see the tiny red dot of Nena's tent.

He took a long, long time to put up his tent. Again and again, the wind almost blew it away. He held it down with his ski sticks and ice axe. Then he pushed his rucksack inside and crawled in after it. But he could not rest. To get water, he had to melt snow with his small stove. His throat hurt, but he had to make himself drink. He was not hungry, but he had to cook and make himself eat. And that night, a storm came up. The temperature fell to −20 °C. Winds of over 80 kilometres per hour tried to blow the tent off the mountain.

Next morning the wind had fallen, but Messner felt terribly tired. For an hour he lay in his tent, half asleep, unable to move. Every small thing – making a drink, eating, putting on his boots – was hard work. He had to argue with himself.

'You must go on,' he told himself. Then, a minute later: 'Why don't I go down?' But he knew the answer to that. 'I wanted to make the climb. I still want to.'

He took the tent down and packed his rucksack. The sky was blue, the sun was shining. But as he set out, the clouds and wind came back. His legs were tired, and his 18 kilogram rucksack seemed heavier than before. Every fifteen steps now, he stopped to rest.

There was too much new snow on the ridge, so he moved down onto the rocky north face – the same way that Norton had gone, also without oxygen. The rocks sloped steeply like the roof on a church. It was very quiet, but Messner began to hear voices. 'Is that somebody talking nearby?' he wondered. 'Is somebody there? . . . I believe I hear voices. Perhaps it is Mallory and Irvine!'

By 3 o'clock in the afternoon he was at 8,220 metres. He was too tired to go on any more. He could only take ten steps now before resting. He found a flat piece of snow above a large rock, and put up his tent there. He took a picture of the tent, then got inside his sleeping bag. Again, he had to melt snow to get water. And it was difficult to sleep. Even when he was resting in the tent, his heart was beating 100 times a minute.

Next morning he could see little – he was in the clouds. Should he go on, or wait, he wondered. No, he thought, he couldn't wait. 'It's now or never. Either-or. I must either go up or go down. There is no other choice.'

Messner's tent

He decided to leave the tent and rucksack behind. He put the camera in his pocket, picked up his ice axe, and set out. It was harder to climb without the ski sticks. He was afraid that he would fall, so he often climbed on hands and knees. As he climbed up to the ridge, it became steeper. Often, he dug his ice axe into the snow above his head, and lay on his face, resting.

For three hours he crawled slowly along the ridge. His dry throat felt like wood. 'Where is the summit?' he wondered. He could see almost nothing. Then, suddenly, the cloud cleared, and he could see right down to the glacier in the valley. He took a few photos, then the cloud came back.

'Where is the summit?' he wondered. 'At most it can only be another ten metres up to the top!' He crawled on, always upwards. Then, suddenly, there it was. The metal tripod, which the Chinese had fixed to the summit in 1975 – it was there in front of him! Messner had seen it before, in 1978; now he took hold of it, like an old friend.

He had done it! He was on top of the world, with nothing above him but sky. He sat down, like a stone. All he wanted to do was rest. But it was after 3 o'clock. He could not stay here in the dark. Slowly, he got up. He took a few photos. Then, at 4 o'clock, he turned to go.

'I must get back down,' he thought. 'Half an hour too late means the end of me.'

On the way down he started coughing badly. When he reached the tent he lay in his sleeping bag like a dead man. But he could not

Messner at the tripod

sleep. He melted a little snow to drink, but ate nothing. Next morning, he left the tent where it was. Carrying the ski sticks and rucksack, he came down the mountain like a man walking in his sleep. Twice he slipped and fell. Each time, he turned on his face and dug his ice axe into the snow.

Then suddenly, on the glacier, he saw Nena standing in front of him. Resting on his ski sticks, he looked at her. Was she really there? Yes, she was.

'Reinhold, how are you?' she said. She ran towards him.

Messner fell to his knees. He was crying. Nena held him in her arms. 'Everything's OK, Reinhold,' she said. 'You are all right. The camp is over there.'

'Where are all my friends?' he asked.

'I'm your friend. I'm here, Reinhold. Don't worry, we're going to our camp now.'

'Yes, where is the camp actually?' he asked.

'Over there.' She took his rucksack, and led him to the camp. Here, she gave him food and drink and let him sleep. All next day he lay in his sleeping bag without moving, while Nena watched over him.

Reinhold Messner had climbed the highest mountain in the world, all alone, with no oxygen. But the mountain had beaten him too. They both won this fight, the mountain and the man.

# 12    The final question

By 1999, many people, both men and women, had climbed Everest. They came from the USA, India, China, Japan, Italy, and many more countries. One climber, Göran Kropp from Sweden, rode his bicycle to Everest, climbed the mountain without oxygen, and rode home again. But still nobody had found an answer to the question: what happened to Mallory and Irvine?

A climber called Jochen Hemmleb became interested in this problem in 1988. He studied the problem for years, and his bedroom was full of books and photos of Everest. But with every new piece of information, there were new questions.

In 1924, Odell was at 7,926 metres, climbing up behind Mallory and Irvine towards Camp 6. At 12.50 p.m. the clouds cleared, and Odell could see the summit ridge of Everest above him. High up on the ridge, he saw two tiny black dots moving on the snow. They were moving quickly. He saw them climb a rock step on the ridge. Then the clouds came back and they disappeared.

There are three rock steps on the north-east ridge: the First Step, the Second Step, and the Third Step. The Second Step is much harder to climb than the First and Third Steps. It is a steep rock wall, like the front of a ship. But it is only about 250 vertical metres from the summit; and the Third Step is even closer. So the first question is: which of the three steps were Mallory and Irvine climbing when Odell last saw them?

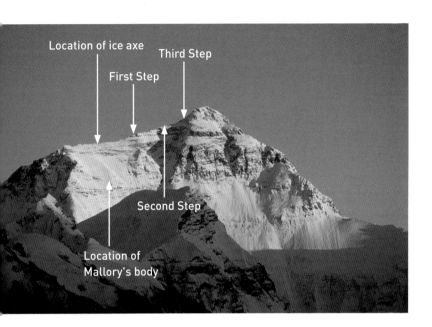

In 1924, Odell said it was the 'rock step at a very short distance from the base of the final pyramid.' And both of them climbed quickly to the top of it. It is difficult to climb the Second Step, but much easier to climb the Third Step. And the First Step is quite a *long* distance from the summit.

So at 12.50 p.m., Mallory and Irvine were probably at either the Second Step or the Third Step – only 'a very short distance' from the summit. If that is right, did they stop there? Probably not. All the difficult parts of the climb were behind them. They had oxygen, and Odell said they were 'moving quickly.'

So did they reach the summit, before they died? Many people think it is quite possible. But others think Odell made a mistake. 'He only saw them for a moment,' they say. 'He probably saw them climb the First Step – much further from the summit.'

Reinhold Messner agrees. 'Mallory did not climb the Second Step,' he says. 'Odell saw them on the First Step.'

So who is right? And how can we know?

In 1933, a British climber found Irvine's ice axe at 8,460 metres, just below the First Step. But why was it there? Did he put it down, or drop it in an accident? And did this happen on the way up, or the way down? No one knows.

In 1960, a Chinese climber found an old wooden tent post and rope, like those used in 1924, just below the Second Step. And in 1979 a Japanese climber met another Chinese climber, Wang Hongbao, on the mountain, and heard a strange story.

Four years earlier, Wang said, he had found a body – 'an English dead' – near the Chinese Camp 6, at 8,100 metres. Was this Mallory, perhaps, or Irvine? The Japanese climber wanted to ask more questions, but the very next day, Wang himself was killed in an avalanche.

So the questions continued. In 1999, Jochen Hemmleb was part of an expedition that set out to find some answers.

From Tibet, they climbed slowly up the East Rongbuk Glacier to Camp 5, just under the North East Ridge. At 7,900 metres, one climber, Andy Politz, reached the place where Odell

The 1999 expedition

had last seen Mallory and Irvine far above him. Where had they actually been, when he saw them? Politz looked up. He could clearly see each of the First, Second and Third Steps.

'You are really close to them at that point,' he said. 'And there was only one place that (was) "a very short distance from the base of the final pyramid", and that was the Third Step – the one nearest the summit.' He took a lot of photographs and video film to make this clear.

The five climbers reached Camp 6, near the place where Wang Hongbao had seen the 'English dead.' On 1 May 1999, they set out to find the body again. They climbed across a steep snow slope, some going up, others down.

It was a dangerous, frightening place. A strong wind made it easy to fall. After half an hour, they had found the bodies of not one but *six* dead climbers. All the dead bodies had broken arms or legs. And the climbers knew that at any moment they could fall and die too, like the men before them.

But the dead bodies wore modern clothes, in bright red or orange colours – very different from the clothes that climbers wore in 1924. Then Conrad Anker saw something white on the rocks below him. He climbed down carefully towards it. Then he called the others on his radio. 'Come down here,' he said. 'Look at this.'

As soon as they saw it, they knew this body was different. This was no modern climber. This man had been here for seventy-five years. Some of his clothes were gone, blown away by the wind, and his skin was white.

There was no oxygen equipment. The rope around his waist had cut into the skin, and was broken at one end where he had fallen. One leg was broken in two places. His head and arms were cut.

They stood and looked at the body quietly for a while. They took photographs. Then, very gently, they began to look in the pockets of the man's clothes.

One thing they hoped to find was a camera. In 1924, when Mallory and Irvine set out for the summit, Somervell gave Mallory a small camera to take with him. Did Mallory take photos at the summit, or not? The camera could give the answer.

In Mallory's pockets they found some sweets, some letters from his brother and sister, a knife, a broken watch, his snow goggles – but no camera. They looked carefully all around, but the camera was not there.

Mallory's things

It was too cold and dangerous to stay there long. But they did not want to leave the body as it was. For all of them, Mallory was a great man – one of the first and bravest of all the men who tried to climb Everest. So, before they left, they decided to bury his body. They covered the body with big stones. Then they said prayers over the body.

They had found one body, but they were still looking for answers. It was clear, though, that Mallory had stopped using oxygen. There was no oxygen equipment on his body, so he probably threw it away when he had used all the oxygen. That means Mallory and Irvine did not turn back early – like Bourdillon and Evans in 1953 – when they still had enough oxygen to get back to Camp 6. Probably they went on, trying to reach the summit even when they knew it was dangerous.

Mallory's snow goggles were in his pocket, so perhaps he was coming down after dark. The broken rope round Mallory's waist shows that the two men were probably still climbing down together. The moon went down early that night, at 11.25 p.m.; after that there was only starlight to help them. They were tired, thirsty, and had no oxygen. But they were only 400 metres from the tiny tent at Camp 6, where Odell had left food. They were almost safe.

And then – something happened. Perhaps something like this.

*They are climbing down together in the dark. Irvine is going first, Mallory is behind. Suddenly, Mallory slips and falls. Irvine tries to save him but the rope breaks. Mallory falls faster and faster. When he hits the ground his leg breaks in two places. But he does not stop. He is sliding down the steep slope, towards the Rongbuk Glacier thousands of feet below. He has dropped his ice axe, but he turns on his face and digs his fingers into the snow above his head, trying to slow down. He stops, but he has hit his head on a rock. He lies there, unable to move, dying alone in the dark.*

*Somewhere far above him, Irvine is injured too. He calls to Mallory, again and again, but there is no answer. Slowly, he tries to crawl towards Camp 6, but he cannot find it. Alone, and lost in the dark and icy cold at 8,200 metres, Irvine dies too.*

Did they reach the summit before they died? Only Mallory's camera can answer that question, and no one has found it.

But there is one other important thing which no one has found. When Mallory left England in 1924, he took a photo of his wife, Ruth, with him. And he made a promise to her, in words like these.

'I'll look at your photo every day. But I will not bring it back. I'm going to take it with me to the summit of Everest. When I get there, I'm going to bury your photograph in the snow, on top of the highest mountain in the world.'

The five climbers searched carefully for the photograph of Mallory's wife in his pockets.

But it was not there.

# GLOSSARY

**attempt**  when you try to do something difficult

**avalanche**  a lot of snow and ice that falls quickly down the side of a mountain

**breathe**  to take air in through your nose or mouth; *(n)* **breath**

**bury**  to put a dead body in the ground

**camp**  a place where people live in tents for a short time

**col**  a narrow path between two higher points in a line of mountains

**collapse**  to fall down suddenly

**cornice**  a pile of snow blown by the wind to make an edge that hangs over the top of a ridge

**cough**  to send air out of your throat with a sudden loud noise

**crawl**  to move slowly on your hands and knees

**crucifix**  a cross with the figure of Jesus Christ on it

**distance**  how far it is from one place to another

**dot**  a small round mark like this .

**equipment**  special things that you need for doing something

**exhausted**  very tired

**expedition**  a journey to do or find something special

**frostbite**  when a part of your body (especially fingers or toes) is damaged by very cold temperatures

**further**  at a greater distance

**get used to**  to become familiar with something that was once new to you

**goddess**  a female spirit that has power over people

**hardly**  almost not; only just

**height**  how high something is

**hobnail**  a short piece of metal put on the bottom of a boot to make it stronger

**knee**  the part in the middle of your leg where it bends

**load**  something that is carried by a person

**melt**  to become liquid after becoming warmer

**monastery** a place where religious men called monks live together; *(n)* **monk**

**oxygen** a gas (O) in the air that people need to live

**planet** the Earth, Mars, and Venus are all planets

**porter** a person whose job is to carry things

**prayer** words that you say when you speak to God or to a god

**pyramid** a shape with three or four sides that come to a point at the top

**ridge** a long narrow edge where two slopes meet.

**sea level** the height of the sea; heights on land are measured from here

**set out** to begin a journey

**shiver** to shake because you are cold

**skyline** the place where the land meets the sky

**slide** (past **slid**) to move easily across something smooth or wet

**slip** to move smoothly over something by accident and fall or nearly fall

**slope** *(n & v)* a piece of ground that has one end higher than the other

**steep** rising quickly

**temperature** how hot or cold something is

**throat** the part inside your neck that takes food and air down from your mouth into your body

**tiny** very small

**tripod** a piece of metal with three legs

**view** what you can see from a place

**waist** the narrow part around the middle of your body

**wool** the soft thick hair of sheep

**yak** an animal of the cow family with long horns and thick hair

Please see Before Reading Activity 1 on page 58 for more vocabulary.

# The Everest Story

## ACTIVITIES

ACTIVITIES

## *Before Reading*

**1 Match the pictures to the definitions.**

1 ☐ a bag that you carry on your back
2 ☐ big glasses which keep the snow or sun out of your eyes
3 ☐ a big warm bag that you sleep in
4 ☐ very thick strong string
5 ☐ long thin pieces of metal to help people move across snow
6 ☐ a small electric light that you can carry
7 ☐ a sharp metal tool used by climbers to cut steps into ice
8 ☐ special things to help you breathe
9 ☐ metal plates which you can put on the bottom of your shoes to help you walk on ice or snow

2  **Now match the pictures to the words.**

1 ☐ crampons
2 ☐ goggles
3 ☐ ice axe
4 ☐ oxygen equipment
5 ☐ rope
6 ☐ rucksack
7 ☐ ski sticks
8 ☐ sleeping bag
9 ☐ torch

3  **Are these sentences true (T) or false (F)?**

1  Everest is between Tibet and Nepal.
2  Everest is the second highest mountain in the world.
3  The name for Everest in the Tibetan language is Chomolungma.
4  Only three climbers have ever died on Everest.
5  Two British people climbed to the top of Everest in 1924 and came back alive.

## ACTIVITIES

# *While Reading*

**Read Chapters 1 and 2, then rewrite these untrue sentences
with the correct information.**

1 The dead man was wearing brightly coloured clothes.
2 The dead man's arm was broken in two places.
3 The dead climber was Andrew Irvine.
4 Everest is 8,155 metres above sea level.
5 Above 900 metres, most people begin to feel ill and tired.
6 Temperatures on Everest often go below −40 °C.
7 The earliest climbers got to Everest through Nepal.

**Read Chapters 3 and 4, then circle *a*, *b* or *c*.**

1 Until _____ century, nobody in the west knew about Everest.
   a. the eighteenth    b. the nineteenth    c. the twentieth
2 George Everest was a British _____ who made maps.
   a. traveller         b. climber           c. soldier
3 In 1921 _____ carried the food, tents, and climbing equipment.
   a. Tibetan porters   b. Tibetan monks    c. British porters
4 In 1921 George Mallory climbed to _____ metres.
   a. 4,800             b. 7,000             c. 8,227
5 The British expedition returned to Everest in 1922 with _____.
   a. oxygen            b. hobnail boots     c. more porters
6 To get water to drink, the climbers _____.
   a. found a river     b. ate snow          c. melted snow
7 In 1922 George Mallory tried to reach the summit _____.
   a. once              b. twice             c. four times
8 In 1922 seven porters were killed by _____.
   a. a rock fall       b. a snow storm      c. an avalanche

**Read Chapters 5, 6, and 7. Fill the gaps with these names. Use some of the names more than once.**

*Bruce, Irvine, Mallory, Namgya, Noel, Norton, Odell, Somervell*

1 _____ was the chief climber on the 1924 expedition.
2 _____ fell into a crevasse and only his ice axe saved him.
3 _____ climbed down and saved two porters in danger.
4 _____ couldn't use his hands because he had frostbite.
5 _____ went with Mallory and the porters to camps 4 and 5.
6 _____ couldn't breathe and coughed up a ball of blood.
7 _____ was young and understood the oxygen equipment.
8 _____ filmed the 1924 expedition.
9 _____ wrote a note to Noel to explain where he was going.
10 _____ was the last person to see Mallory and Irvine alive.

**Read Chapters 8 and 9, then answer these questions.**

1 After 1950, which country did Everest climbers go through?
2 Who was Tenzing? When did he first try to climb Everest?
3 What is the Khumbu Icefall? Why is it so dangerous?
4 What did Lowe and Annullu do for eleven days?
5 Why did Bourdillon and Evans turn back in 1953? Why was it the right thing to do?
6 What did Bourdillon and Evans look like on their return?

**Read Chapter 10. Choose the best question word for these questions, and then answer them.**

*How / What / Who / Why*

1 _____ carried heavy loads of 27 kilograms to Camp 9?
2 _____ was the weather like for the climb to the summit?
3 _____ high was the rock wall near the summit?
4 _____ did Hillary and Tenzing do at the summit?
5 _____ did they leave the summit after only fifteen minutes?

**Read Chapter 11. Put these events in the correct order.**

1 Messner returned to Everest two years later with his girlfriend, Nena.

2 Messner and Nena climbed back up to Camp 3. After two days he packed his rucksack and said goodbye to Nena.

3 Messner came down and saw Nena once again. He fell to his knees and cried.

4 Messner and Habeler climbed Everest without any oxygen.

5 An hour later Messner fell into a crevasse and nearly died.

6 At last Messner reached the summit, alone and without oxygen.

7 Messner climbed further and put up his tent at 7,800 and then at 8,220 metres.

8 Messner climbed up to the North Col but then came down and spent three weeks walking above 5,000 metres.

**Read Chapter 12, then match these halves of sentences.**

1 Jochen Hemmleb wanted to know the true story of . . .

2 In 1924 Mallory and Irvine were last seen by . . .

3 In 1933 a British climber found Irvine's . . .

4 In the 1970s a dead body was seen by . . .

5 The expedition in 1999 found Mallory's . . .

6 They also found Mallory's knife and his . . .

7 Nobody knows Mallory's story because they can't find his . . .

a a Chinese climber called Wang Hongbao.

b body.

c camera.

d Mallory and Irvine.

e ice axe.

f snow goggles.

g Odell.

ACTIVITIES

## *After Reading*

1 Find these words in the wordsearch below, and draw lines through them. They go from left to right, and top to bottom.

*avalanche, breathe, cough, crawl, dot, exhausted, frostbite, knee, load, oxygen, melt, rope, rucksack, shiver, slip, steep, temperature, throat, torch*

| C | O | U | G | H | T | H | R | O | A | T |
|---|---|---|---|---|---|---|---|---|---|---|
| E | G | O | D | B | D | E | O | X | S | C |
| X | S | L | M | R | O | R | P | Y | S | R |
| H | T | O | S | E | K | U | E | G | H | A |
| A | V | A | L | A | N | C | H | E | I | W |
| U | H | D | I | T | E | K | E | N | V | L |
| S | R | O | P | H | E | S | F | T | E | M |
| T | E | M | P | E | R | A | T | U | R | E |
| E | H | E | T | O | R | C | H | W | O | L |
| D | S | T | E | E | P | K | R | D | O | T |
| F | R | O | S | T | B | I | T | E | L | D |

Now write down all the letters that do not have lines through them, beginning with the first line and going across each line to the end. You now have 23 letters, which make a phrase of 5 words.

– What does the phrase describe?
– Who uses the phrase?

Look back at the words at the top of the page. Make sentences about the problems that climbers have on Everest.

**2 Fill in the gaps in the newspaper article with these words.**

*bodies / British / didn't / disappeared / discovered / down /
first / highest / last / letters / modern / pockets / reach /
return / set out / seventy-five / shirt / six / stand / steep / two / up*

---

# FAMOUS _____ CLIMBER
# FOUND ON EVEREST

The body of George Mallory was found on Everest
yesterday, _____ years after he suddenly _____. An
expedition _____ Mallory's body on a _____ snow slope
near the summit of the world's _____ mountain.

Mallory was _____ seen climbing _____ towards the
top of Everest with Andrew Irvine. But the two men
didn't _____ to camp and their _____ were never found.
For many years people have asked one question: Were
Mallory and Irvine the _____ climbers to _____ on the
summit of Everest?

The new expedition of five men wanted to answer
that question and they _____ to look for Mallory
and Irvine's bodies. At first, they found _____ dead
climbers all in _____ coloured clothes. But then, they
saw another body with clothes and equipment from the
1920s. This dead climber was lying face _____ and his
leg was broken in _____ places. They looked inside his
_____ and found a name – it was George Mallory.

Inside Mallory's _____ they found some sweets and
_____, a knife, a watch and some snow goggles. But
they _____ find his camera. Without this we will never
know the one most important thing: did Mallory and
Irvine _____ the summit of Everest?

---

3 You are going to climb Everest with a partner. You have
a tent, food, and clothes, but you must also choose some
climbing equipment (look back at pages 58 and 59). Answer
the questions below and explain your ideas to the class.

- Which five pieces of equipment will you take with you?
- Why are these pieces of equipment important?
- What one extra thing would you like to take?

4 Do you agree or disagree with these sentences? Why?

1 Reaching the summit of Everest is the most exciting thing
that any climber can do.
2 Some climbers have only thought about themselves and
they haven't looked after the Tibetan or Nepalese porters.
3 The Tibetan and Nepalese porters are often forgotten in
the famous stories about Everest.
4 Modern climbers leave too much rubbish on Everest.
They need to take more care of the world's most famous
mountain.
5 A lot of people want to climb Everest now. But only a small
number of people should climb the mountain every year.

5 Find out about another person who climbed Everest. It could
be the youngest climber, first woman, or the first person from
your country. Give a talk to your class about it. Websites like
www.everestnews.com and www.mnteverest.net will give you
more information.

Use these questions to help you.
- What was the climber's age, nationality, and climbing
experience?
- When did they climb Everest, who with, by which route,
and how long did they take?
- What problems did they have?

# ABOUT THE AUTHOR

Tim Vicary was born in London in 1949. He attended Cambridge University and then worked as a schoolteacher, and is now a teaching fellow at the Norwegian Study Centre at the University of York. He is married, has two children, and lives in the country in Yorkshire, in the north of England. He has written coursebooks for use in Norwegian secondary schools, and has also published two historical novels, *The Blood Upon the Rose,* and *Cat and Mouse,* under his own name, and a crime novel, *A Game of Proof,* under the pseudonym Megan Stark. He has not climbed Everest, but as a young man he took a bicycle to the top of Snowdon, a mountain in North Wales. Fortunately, his attempts to ride down the mountain stopped before he did serious damage to himself.

He has written about 20 books for Oxford Bookworms, from Starter to Stage 3. His other Oxford Bookworms titles at Stage 1 are *The Coldest Place on Earth* (True Stories), *The Elephant Man* (True Stories), *Mary, Queen of Scots* (True Stories), *The Murder of Mary Jones* (Playscripts), *Mutiny on the Bounty* (True Stories), *Pocahontas* (True Stories), and *White Death* (Thriller and Adventure). His website is www.timvicary.com.

# OXFORD BOOKWORMS LIBRARY

*Classics • Crime & Mystery • Factfiles • Fantasy & Horror*
*Human Interest • Playscripts • Thriller & Adventure*
*True Stories • World Stories*

The OXFORD BOOKWORMS LIBRARY provides enjoyable reading in English, with a wide range of classic and modern fiction, non-fiction, and plays. It includes original and adapted texts in seven carefully graded language stages, which take learners from beginner to advanced level. An overview is given on the next pages.

All Stage 1 titles are available as audio recordings, as well as over eighty other titles from Starter to Stage 6. All Starters and many titles at Stages 1 to 4 are specially recommended for younger learners. Every Bookworm is illustrated, and Starters and Factfiles have full-colour illustrations.

The OXFORD BOOKWORMS LIBRARY also offers extensive support. Each book contains an introduction to the story, notes about the author, a glossary, and activities. Additional resources include tests and worksheets, and answers for these and for the activities in the books. There is advice on running a class library, using audio recordings, and the many ways of using Oxford Bookworms in reading programmes. Resource materials are available on the website <www.oup.com/bookworms>.

The *Oxford Bookworms Collection* is a series for advanced learners. It consists of volumes of short stories by well-known authors, both classic and modern. Texts are not abridged or adapted in any way, but carefully selected to be accessible to the advanced student.

You can find details and a full list of titles in the *Oxford Bookworms Library Catalogue* and *Oxford English Language Teaching Catalogues*, and on the website <www.oup.com/bookworms>.

## THE OXFORD BOOKWORMS LIBRARY
## GRADING AND SAMPLE EXTRACTS

### STARTER • 250 HEADWORDS

present simple – present continuous – imperative –
*can/cannot, must – going to* (future) – simple gerunds ...

Her phone is ringing – but where is it?

Sally gets out of bed and looks in her bag. No phone. She looks under the bed. No phone. Then she looks behind the door. There is her phone. Sally picks up her phone and answers it. *Sally's Phone*

### STAGE 1 • 400 HEADWORDS

... past simple – coordination with *and, but, or* – subordination with *before, after, when, because, so* ...

I knew him in Persia. He was a famous builder and I worked with him there. For a time I was his friend, but not for long. When he came to Paris, I came after him – I wanted to watch him. He was a very clever, very dangerous man. *The Phantom of the Opera*

### STAGE 2 • 700 HEADWORDS

... present perfect – *will* (future) – *(don't) have to, must not, could* – comparison of adjectives – simple *if* clauses – past continuous – tag questions – *ask/tell* + infinitive ...

While I was writing these words in my diary, I decided what to do. I must try to escape. I shall try to get down the wall outside. The window is high above the ground, but I have to try. I shall take some of the gold with me – if I escape, perhaps it will be helpful later. *Dracula*

## STAGE 3 • 1000 HEADWORDS

*… should, may* – present perfect continuous – *used to* – past perfect –
causative – relative clauses – indirect statements …

Of course, it was most important that no one should see Colin,
Mary, or Dickon entering the secret garden. So Colin gave orders
to the gardeners that they must all keep away from that part of
the garden in future. *The Secret Garden*

## STAGE 4 • 1400 HEADWORDS

… past perfect continuous – passive (simple forms) –
*would* conditional clauses – indirect questions –
relatives with *where/when* – gerunds after prepositions/phrases …

I was glad. Now Hyde could not show his face to the world
again. If he did, every honest man in London would be proud
to report him to the police. *Dr Jekyll and Mr Hyde*

## STAGE 5 • 1800 HEADWORDS

… future continuous – future perfect –
passive (modals, continuous forms) –
*would have* conditional clauses – modals + perfect infinitive …

If he had spoken Estella's name, I would have hit him. I was so
angry with him, and so depressed about my future, that I could
not eat the breakfast. Instead I went straight to the old house.
*Great Expectations*

## STAGE 6 • 2500 HEADWORDS

… passive (infinitives, gerunds) – advanced modal meanings –
clauses of concession, condition

When I stepped up to the piano, I was confident. It was as if I
knew that the prodigy side of me really did exist. And when I
started to play, I was so caught up in how lovely I looked that
I didn't worry how I would sound. *The Joy Luck Club*

BOOKWORMS · FACTFILES · STAGE 1
# Titanic
TIM VICARY

On a quiet sea, the biggest ship in the world is waiting. There is no noise from the engines. Up in the night sky there are hundreds of stars. Behind the ship, an iceberg – a great mountain of ice – goes slowly away into the black night.

In the beautiful first-class rooms rich passengers eat and listen to music. Down in the third-class cabins, families sleep. An exciting new life is waiting for them in America.

But for many of the people in this small 'city on the sea', this is their last night alive . . .

BOOKWORMS · FACTFILES · STAGE 2
# Ireland
TIM VICARY

There are many different Irelands. There is the Ireland of peaceful rivers, green fields, and beautiful islands. There is the Ireland of song and dance, pubs and theatres – the country of James Joyce, Bob Geldof, and Riverdance. And there is the Ireland of guns, fighting, death, and the hope of peace. Come with us and visit all of these Irelands – and many more . . .

BOOKWORMS · FACTFILES · STAGE 2

# The Beautiful Game

STEVE FLINDERS

Some call it football, some call it soccer, and to others it's 'the beautiful game'. By any name, it's a sport with some fascinating stories. There is murder in Colombia, and a game that lasts for two days where many players never see the ball. There's the French writer who learnt lessons about life from playing football, and the women players who had to leave the club grounds because 'Women's football isn't nice'.

The cups, the leagues, the World Cup finals, the stars, the rules – they're all a part of the world's favourite sport, the beautiful game.

BOOKWORMS · FACTFILES · STAGE 3

# Australia and New Zealand

CHRISTINE LINDOP

What do you find in these two countries at the end of the world? One is an enormous island, where only twenty million people live – and the other is two long, narrow islands, with ten sheep for every person. One country has the biggest rock in all the world, and a town where everybody lives under the ground. The other has a beach where you can sit beside the sea in a pool of hot water, and lakes that are bright yellow, green, and blue.

Open this book and start your journey – to two countries where something strange, beautiful or surprising waits around every corner.

BOOKWORMS · FACTFILES · STAGE 3

# The USA

ALISON BAXTER

Everybody knows about the United States. You can see its films, hear its music, and eat its food just about everywhere in the world. Cowboys, jazz, hamburgers, the Stars and Stripes – that's the United States.

But it's a country with many stories to tell. Stories of busy cities, and quiet, beautiful forests and parks. Stories of a country that fought against Britain, and then against itself, to make the United States of today. Stories of rich and poor, black and white, Native American and immigrant. And the story of what it is really like to be an American today . . .

BOOKWORMS · FACTFILES · STAGE 3

# Martin Luther King

ALAN C. McLEAN

The United States in the 1950s and 60s was a troubled place. Black people were angry, because they did not have the same rights as whites. It was a time of angry words, of marches, of protests, a time of bombs and killings.

But above the angry noise came the voice of one man – a man of peace. 'I have a dream,' said Martin Luther King, and it was a dream of blacks and whites living together in peace and freedom. This is the story of an extraordinary man, who changed American history in his short life.